DATE DUE			

HISTORY OF ROCK AND ROLL

Rock in Retrospect —

THE 1980s

Written by: Stuart A. Kallen
Edited by: Bob Italia

1

Published by Abdo & Daughters, 6537 Cecilia Circle, Bloomington, Minnesota 55435

Library bound edition distributed by Rockbottom Books, Pentagon Tower, P.O. Box 36036, Minneapolis, Minnesota 55435

Library of Congress Number: 89-084919   ISBN: 0-939179-77-6

Cover Photos by: Michael Ochs Archive
Inside Photos by: Michael Ochs Archive

INTRODUCTION

As the 1980's fade into history, Rock-n-Roll is bigger than ever. Rock-n-Roll will have its 35th birthday in 1990. If Elvis were alive he would be 55 years old. It's hard to imagine a grey-haired, 48-year-old Jimi Hendrix lighting his guitar on fire!

As always, new technology pushes Rock-n-Roll into the future. The amazing sound quality of Compact Discs (CD's) has allowed us to hear music from the 50s and the 60s with new ears. Because of digital remixing, the music of everyone from Chuck Berry to the Beatles sounds better now than it did when it was released.

STILL ROCKIN' AROUND THE CLOCK

Television, the instrument that brought us Elvis Presley in the 50s and the Beatles in the 60s, still led the Rock Revolution in the 80s. On August 1, 1981, MTV started broadcasting music videos 24-hours a day. MTV revived the careers of faltering bands like Heart and Z.Z. Top, and cemented the Superstar status of people like Bruce Springsteen and Michael Jackson. For the first time, an entire T.V. channel was dedicated to the sole purpose of playing Rock around the clock! Television, combined with satellites in outer space, brought 1.5 billion people together for the Live Aid concert.

Black music from Africa and Jamaica made some premiere appearances in the 80s. Paul Simon played with a band from South Africa on "Graceland," and Bob Marley's Jamaican Reggae beat can be heard in the music of everyone from Blondie to The Police to Prince.

As we pass into the 21st century and beyond, Rock music can be found in every corner of the globe and even in outerspace as Pink Floyd sent their music along on a space probe!

THE NEW WAVE —
PUNK GROWS UP

In the late 70s, bands like the Sex Pistols and the Clash self-destructed in the violent atmosphere they had created. But the ideas put forth by Punk Rockers were taken one step further by people of broader talent and vision. Elvis Costello, the Cars and the Pretenders are all examples of people who took the no-nonsense approach to music. Their music used stripped down arrangements and basic honesty to climb into the Top 10. The growth of small, independent college radio stations gave many New Wave bands airplay that they otherwise would not have had.

BLONDIE —
NEW WAVE'S NUMBER ONE

Back in 1976, when Madonna was an unknown 16-year-old, Blondie's front-woman, Debbie Harry, was revolutionizing the role of women in popular music. Performing at the Punk club CBGB's, dressed in an array of outrageous outfits, thrashing her bottle-blonde hair, Debbie Harry was the Punk pin-up queen. Besides her Marilyn Monroe good looks, Harry is a talented songwriter who wrote, with guitarist Chris Stein, the Blondie hits that have sold over 50 million records world wide.

Blondie grew out of the Punk scene that was centered in one of the poorest neighborhoods in New York City, the Bowery on the Lower East Side. Along with Patti Smith, the Ramones and the Talking Heads, Blondie is one of the "Class of '77" that took New Wave music out of the New York Bowery and into the Pop mainstream.

After the release of "Heart of Glass" in 1979, Blondie became (temporarily) one of the most successful bands in the world. Combining Surf Music, Girl Group Music, Punk, Rap and Reggae with Harry's pin-up girl good looks, Blondie had a string of platinum hits. "Dreaming," "Call Me" and "The Tide is High" were all huge sellers in the U.S. and England. And white America heard Rap Music for the first time on the Blondie hit, "Rapture."

Tired of the music business, and with their popularity waning, Blondie called it quits in 1983. Debbie appeared in the movies "Videodrome" and "Hairspray" and released several solo albums.

Blondie was the first band to cross over from Punk to Pop. Debbie Harry paved the way for other Pop Princesses like Madonna and Cindi Lauper. Blondie also paved the way for black Reggae and Rap Music by getting it heard on Top 40 radio. Not a bad record for a group of Punks from the Lower East Side.

THE TALKING HEADS — THE THINKING MAN'S NEW WAVE

Does the nine piece band on stage look the way bands will look in the 21st century? Men, women, black, white. Everyone equal in a Rock Democracy.

Dressed in an oversized suit, Adam's apple bobbing up and down, bug-eyed David Byrne, lead singer of the Talking Heads, sings songs about life and death with humor and style. At the fierce, rhythmic height of "Burning Down the House," Byrne starts running in place, then jogging across the stage, behind the drum riser, round and round. The two female back-up vocalists follow, and soon everyone in the audience is running in place as the rest of the band hammers out the African rhythms. This is the state of the Talking Heads in their 1983 movie, "Stop Making Sense."

The Talking Heads were another of the "Class of '77" at CBGB's in New York. David Byrne, guitar and vocals, Chris Frantz, drum and Tina Weymouth, bass, met while students at the Rhode Island School of Design. Adding Jerry Harrison on keys rounded out the Talking Heads line-up.

"When we began, we felt there was this very big hole," said David Byrne in 1978. "We felt, nobody's doing anything for our crowd, we'll have to do it ourselves."

So the Talking Heads set about fusing together complex African rhythms with intelligent lyrics, and New Wave attitudes with Pop melodies. The success of "Stop Making Sense," "Remaining in Light" and "Speaking With Tongues" show that the world was ready for the Talking Heads brand of music. MTV is the perfect medium for the Talking Heads' clever and arty video works. "Burning Down the House" went to number 9 on the U.S. charts, thanks in part to the video play it got on MTV.

Although the Talking Heads are not superstars, they sell enough records to stay afloat in the competitive music business. The Talking Heads are one of the pioneers of New Wave music that speaks to your mind while it's making you dance.

THE POLICE —
FROM PUNK ROOTS TO MEGA-STARDOM

"The Beatles were the biggest band of all," says Sting, the lead singer of The Police. "And we set out to beat them."

Most bands want to be bigger than the Beatles, but most bands find out that it isn't that easy. Most bands except The Police. In their five years together, The Police sold more records than the Beatles did in their entire career. "You're either the best or you're not," says Sting.

THE BUMBLEBEE STINGS

The Police were formed when drummer Stewart Copeland left the band Curved Air. Copeland had witnessed the Punk Revolution in London, and wanted to form a band with catchy melodies fused with Punk simplicity.

Copeland recruited Gordon Sumner on bass. Sumner's nickname was Sting because the black and yellow jacket that he wore looked like a bumblebee. Copeland and Sting added Andy Summers from the Animals on guitar, and started playing the Punk clubs around London.

EVERY LITTLE THING
STING DOES IS MAGIC

Using the Jamaican Reggae beat made famous by Bob Marley, and combining it with Rock and Jazz, The Police had a hit with "Roxanne" in 1979.

After that, there was no stopping The Police. After completing ten tours of Europe and America, The Police had sold five million singles and two million albums. In January of 1980, The Police played 37 cities in 19 countries over four continents in 80 days!

The album "Zenyatta Mondatta" was released in 1981 and became the first Police million seller in the U.S. In January of 1981, The Police became the first New Wave band to play Madison Square Garden in New York City. "Ghost in the Machine" was their second million seller, and "Synchronicity" sold 11 million worldwide. In March of 1984, The Police won four Grammy Awards.

THE DREAM OF THE BLUE TURTLES

All the while insisting that they were **not** breaking up, after 1984, The Police went their separate ways. Sting starred in several movies including the

10

THE POLICE: (L to R) Sting, Stewart Copeland, Andy Summers.

11

science fiction blockbuster "Dune." Sting released "The Dream of the Blue Turtles" in 1985 and it sold as well as The Police records.

While the other members of The Police have faded from the public eye, Sting has become one of the most visible fundraisers for charities in the 80's. Using his talent and popularity, Sting has raised millions of dollars for Amnesty International, a worldwide organization trying to bring basic human rights to many developing countries, where people are imprisoned and tortured for speaking their minds. Sting also is raising millions to save the endangered rain forests in Brazil, an extremely important environmental cause.

Although The Police set out to be the biggest rock stars in the world, they have used their music throughout their careers to feed the children and protect the earth's ecology. As Sting says, "We can sing and dance and save the world!"

BRUCE SPRINGSTEEN — BABY WE WERE BORN TO NUMBER ONE

The searing opening chords to "Rosalita" fly out of Danny Frederici's organ. The rest of Bruce Springsteen's E Street Band pick up the frantic

Bruce Springsteen, Born to Rock.

pace, and the man who saved Rock-n-Roll, Bruce Springsteen, grabs the mic. As Bruce starts to sing, 200,000 eyeballs in the audience are riveted on the Rock God from Jersey. Bruce leads the band on the manic journey through "Rosalita," his eyes popping out, his neck chords bulging with the effort.

As the song reaches its climax, Springsteen climbs up on the drum riser, then on top of the amplifiers. After grabbing his famous Telecaster for a few hot licks, Springsteen jumps off the amplifiers. Can the love of 100,000 fans make him fly? Not tonight, but tomorrow, who knows? Bruce lands on his knees, and skids past Clarence Clemons' searing saxophone, back to where he was born to be — centerstage. As the finale of "Rosalita" fades into the summer sky, thousands of fists punch the air, and thousands of vocal chords chant, "Bruce, Bruce, Bruce, Bruce." The show is over, but the cheering and shouting goes on for another half an hour.

Bruce Frederick Springsteen was born on September 23, 1949 in Freehold, New Jersey. Bruce was a loner throughout his school years, and from the time he was 12, Bruce spent most of his waking hours up in his room, practicing his guitar.

14

Like a million teenagers inspired by Elvis Presley, Bruce spent his teen years bouncing from one band to another. Springsteen played the clubs that dot the shore of Asbury Park, New Jersey, a depressed tourist town on the Atlantic Ocean. During this period, Bruce first played with some members of what would become the E Street Band: Guitarist Miami Steve Van Zant, keyboardist David Sancious, saxophonist Clarence Clemons and bassist Garry Tallent.

THE NEXT BOB DYLAN?

In 1972, Bruce signed a contract with Mike Appel. The contract was signed at night, on the hood of a car, and it gave Appel a huge percentage of Bruce's music income. At the time there was no income. To hear Bruce tell it, "I was writing songs like a madman, I had no money, no where to go, nothing to do. It was cold and I wrote a lot. And I got to feeling very guilty if I didn't."

Appel got Springsteen a contract with Columbia Records, the company that Bob Dylan recorded for. The comparisons to Dylan were immediate. Columbia tried the "next Dylan" strategy on Springsteen's first album, "Greetings From Asbury Park N.J." Showcasing Bruce's words

Bruce Springsteen a compelling performer.

16

instead of his Rock-n-Roll, "Asbury Park" sold 20,000 copies. Not many, but the critics **loved** it.

THE FUTURE OF ROCK-N-ROLL

Things were not going well for Bruce at Columbia. He refused to talk to reporters, he wouldn't warm up for another band. He had to headline wherever he played, and he spent $10,000 recording one song — "Born to Run." Superstars can get away with such behavior, but Springsteen's second album "The Wild, the Innocent and The E-Street Shuffle," had sold only 50,000 copies. It looked like Bruce Springsteen was going to disappear into the black hole of the music industry. That is, until a review of one of Bruce's concerts appeared in a Boston newspaper. After seeing Bruce perform, one of the most important rock critics on the East Coast, John Landau, wrote, "I have seen the future of Rock-n-Roll. Its name is Bruce Springsteen." By 1975, Landau was helping Springsteen produce the album "Born to Run." By 1976 he was Bruce's manager.

"Born to Run" put Bruce at Number One. Several weeks after its release, Bruce Springsteen was featured on the covers of Newsweek magazine and Time magazine on the same day! Only presidents and kings can claim the honor of being featured on the cover of America's two top news magazines during the same week. In 1983, politicians jumped on the Springsteen bandwagon, trying (unsuccessfully) to make "Born to Run" the official song of the state of New Jersey! Bruce shied away from all the publicity, saying, "the music is what's important."

"THE RIVER" DELIVERS

By October of 1980, Bruce Springsteen was the king of Rock-n-Roll. His three-hour-long concerts attracted millions of people and his records went platinum in days. In the void left by Disco music, Springsteen filled in with honest to goodness Rock. The two record set "The River" was released and the single "Hungry Heart" reached Number One. "The River" proved that stardom hadn't changed Bruce. He was still singing anthems about the troubles of the common working man.

BORN IN THE U.S.A.

Springsteen released "Nebraska," and surprised his fans with an entire album of songs featuring just Bruce, his guitar and his harmonica. The haunting songs on "Nebraska" show Springsteen examining complex human emotions and the lives of people driven to desperation. The music was a departure from Bruce's high energy Rock. The words set the tone for Springsteen's growing interest in solving society's problems.

Back in the studio, Bruce was once again "writing like a madman." Bruce wrote and recorded sixty songs, some of which would become "Born in the U.S.A." Featuring the updated studio technology of the mid-1980s, "Born in the U.S.A." sold 6.5 million copies by 1985. The video of the song became a MTV favorite for months.

TUNNEL OF LOVE

As Springsteen's popularity grows, so do his efforts to help the poor and disadvantaged. Bruce played benefits for Viet Nam Veterans, local food shelves and in 1985 he sang on "We Are the World." In the late 80s Bruce has donated his time to stopping the spread of nuclear weapons, to Amnesty International and environmental causes.

In 1987, Bruce released "Tunnel of Love," an album whose themes center on the thoughts and feelings of a more worldly and mature person. His "Tunnel of Love Tour" in 1988 played to smaller audiences, but as usual, the tickets were sold-out in hours. And Bruce still "brought the house down" with hits like "Rosalita," and a slow, acoustic version of "Born to Run."

Bruce Springsteen has sung his songs for millions of people, and made more money than most people can even imagine. But through it all, Bruce remained true to himself and his music. In the mid-seventies, when faceless disco music and super slick marketing dominated the airwaves, Bruce Springsteen gave listeners something honest, that they could believe in. It is that basic honesty that has carried Rock-n-Roll through the years. Bruce Springsteen is truly the Boss of Rock-n-Roll.

LIVE AID —
CONCERT TO FEED THE CHILDREN

"This is your Woodstock!" With those words spoken by Joan Baez, the Live Aid Concert began on July 13, 1985. Live Aid took place at

JFK Stadium in Philadelphia and at Wembly Stadium in London. The seventeen hour concert was tied together with satellites, and was broadcast to 1.5 billion people in 140 countries! The concert was the brainchild of Bob Geldof, founder of the Irish band Boomtown Rats. Live Aid raised over $100 million to feed starving people in Africa.

Live Aid also offered many superstars the chance to jam with each other. Bob Dylan played with members of the Rolling Stones, Sting played with Dire Straits, and Led Zeppelin reuinted with the late John Bonham's son on drums.

Here are some of the supterstars that gave their time and energy to Live Aid: Paul McCartney, David Bowie, Phil Collins, B.B. King, U2, Bob Dylan, Neil Young, Crosby, Stills & Nash, Eric Clapton, The Who, Keith Richards, The Cars, Madonna, Duran Duran, Led Zeppelin, The Pretenders, Adam Ant, INXS, Elvis Costello, Sting, Run DMC, Judas Priest, Dire Straits, Mick Jagger, Elton John, Tom Petty, Tina Turner and more.

Live Aid made visible to the world the fact that Rock-n-Roll can be a mighty resource in bringing people together in order to help those less fortunate.

Michael with the worlds greatest music and film producers, Quincy Jones and Steven Spielberg.

When Bob Dylan said, "We should do this to help our struggling farmers," Willie Nelson picked up the cue and organized Farm Aid in America. Farm Aid featured American Country and Rock musicians and raised millions for American farmers. Once again Rock music helped rescue people that had fallen on hard times.

MICHAEL JACKSON — THRILLER OF MILLIONS

Michael Jackson is far and away the most popular artist of the 80s. The album "Thriller" has sold over 40 million copies, and it is the **best selling record of all time!** Jackson's videos are mini-movies produced by Hollywoods finest talent, and his face can be seen on posters all over the world.

Michael Jackson was born on August 29, 1958. Michael grew up in a small house in Gary, Indiana. His father, Joe Jackson, worked as a crane operator in a steelmill. Joe was also a guitar player who gigged on weekends with a band called the Falcons.

Joe's guitar was strictly off limits to his kids, but Michael's brothers Tito, Jackie and Jermaine would sneak Joe's guitar into their room and play it. One day, Tito broke a string on the guitar, and when Joe came home, the kids prepared themselves for punishment. Instead, Joe asked Tito to show him what he knew. Tito was good, and soon Jackie, Jermaine and Tito began rehearsing together. When Michael was five years old, he joined in with the boys as lead singer.

One day, Joe brought home a shiny red guitar for Tito to play. Within months, the Jackson's house was filled with guitars, drums, microphones, amplifiers and speakers. Joe Jackson rehearsed his children constantly, and if they messed up they got hit with a belt. There was never any time for play, and Micheal remembers sadly that he wished he could play like other kids.

THE JACKSON FIVE

With the addition of Marlon Jackson, the group became known as the Jackson 5. Joe Jackson started entering his kids in talent shows in Gary and nearby Chicago. The audiences were dazzled by the eight-year-old Michael, and the Jackson's were met with success everywhere they played. Soon, the Jackson 5 had their own record out on a small label, and they were playing regularly at clubs in Chicago. Instead of being concerned with school and play like normal eight year olds, Michael was singing and dancing in bars. Michael says that he witnessed some wild and crazy behavior in those bars, things that many **adults** have never seen.

After winning every talent show they could find in Chicago, the Jackson's headed for New York City to enter the talent show at the Apollo Theater. The Apollo is **the** showcase for black artists, and the audiences have been known to boo and throw things at performers they didn't like. Of course, the Jackson 5 won the talent show at the Apollo, and soon they had a date to play The David Frost Show, a very popular T.V. show.

THE BIG BREAK

The Jackson's were back home, getting ready to play on T.V., and the phone rang. After Joe set down the receiver, he said that they had to cancel their T.V. appearance. The Jackson's were stunned, and when they asked why, Joe said with a smile, that Motown Records had just called, and the Jackson 5 had to go to Detroit for an audition! David Frost would have to wait!

The Jackson 5 passed the audition for Motown with flying colors. Motown's founder, Berry Gordy, told the Jackson's that they were going to be the biggest band **in the world!** Michael said it was like a fairy tale come true. And the Jackson 5 rewarded Gordy by having three Number One hits in a row. Michael Jackson was on his way to becoming the biggest star in the world.

EASY AS A-B-C

After the release of "ABC" in 1970, the Jackson's moved to Hollywood where Michael struck up his lifelong friendship with Diana Ross of the Supremes. The Jackson's toured the world and were met with screaming, hysterical fans everywhere they went. There was even a cartoon show called "The Jackson Five." In 1971, Michael did his first solo record, "Got To Be There." In 1972, Michael recorded his first solo album, "Ben."

As the Jackson's grew older, their popularity started sliding. Working within a family structure was not easy for Michael. Around the time of his 21st birthday, Michael quit letting his father manage his career. As Michael says, "Firing your father isn't easy." The Jackson 5 also left Motown Records and went to Epic. Jermaine stayed at Motown and Michael's younger brother, Randy, joined the Jackson 5.

OFF THE WALL

In 1979, Michael recorded the album "Off The Wall" with Quincy Jones as producer. After its release it became the biggest selling album by a black artist, ever. "Off The Wall" also yielded three singles in the Top 10 — all at the same time!

While Michael was very popular with record buyers, he says that this period of his life was very lonely for him. "The things I share with millions of people aren't the sort of things you share with one," says Michael. "I believe I'm one of the loneliest people in the world."

THRILLER

Ever since Michael was a little boy he had a dream — to make the biggest selling album of all time. After selling six million copies of "Off The Wall," Michael went back into the studio with

Quincy Jones and recorded "Thriller." After much exhausting work, "Thriller" was released and Michael's dream came true. At 40 million copies, "The Guinness Book of World Records" lists "Thriller" as the biggest selling album of all time! At one point, Michael was selling one million records a week.

"THRILLER" — KILLER VIDEOS

Michael was disappointed with many of the videos he saw on MTV, and when it came time to make videos for "Thriller," he wanted to make the highest quality videos possible.

Because "Beat It" is a song about street gangs, Michael went to the rough streets of Los Angeles and rounded up some real life gang members to appear in his video. After working with these so-called tough guys, Michael realized that they were lonely people looking for attention, just like himself. They only wanted to be "somebody" and Michael made friends with several of them.

The videos "Billie Jean," "Beat It" and "Thriller" all became Number One videos, and set the standards for high-quality, well produced video. Michael won seven Grammy Awards for "Thriller" including Best Album of the Year.

A TRAGIC ACCIDENT

In January of 1984, Michael Jackson was one of the most famous people in the world. The Jackson's agreed to do a commercial for Pepsi-Cola, and Michael was to be filmed descending a stairway as flash-bombs went off behind him. On the fourth "take" of the scene, something went wrong. As Michael danced down the stairs, the flash-bombs went off on either side of his head. But a spark landed in Michael's hair. Michael's head was suddenly on fire! The movie set fell into chaos as Michael fell to the floor screaming.

An ambulance took Michael to the hospital where he was treated for the third-degree burns that almost went through to his skull. The doctors told Michael that if his clothes would have caught on fire, he probably would have died.

After the accident, Michael signed a record setting $14 million contract with Pepsi, which earned him another entry in "The Guinness Book of World Records." Michael also donated $1.5 million to charity for burn victims.

WE ARE THE WORLD

When Michael had recovered from his accident, he reunited with his family for The Jackson's Victory Tour. Michael didn't want to do it, but performing with his family again made him happy. The Victory Tour was just like the old days, with screaming fans surrounding their hotels and sold out stadiums in every town. Michael donated the entire $4 million he made on the tour to charities.

In 1985, after watching news footage of starving people in Ethiopia, Michael wrote "We Are The World" with Lionel Richie. 45 artists sang on "We Are The World" including Bob Dylan, Ray Charles, The Jackson's, Billy Joel, Cyndi Lauper, Huey Lewis, Bette Midler, Willie Nelson, the Pointer Sisters, Paul Simon, Bruce Springsteen, Tina Turner and Stevie Wonder.

On April 5, 1985, at 3:50 P.M. Greenwich Mean Time, 5000 radio stations in countries all around the world, including China, Africa, and East Germany, played "We Are The World." A year after its release, "We Are The World" raised over $44 million which was sent to Africa to feed the starving people. Michael Jackson can take credit for saving thousands of lives.

Michael recording "We Are The World."

THE MAN IN THE MIRROR

After working hard for several years on a new album, in 1987, Michael released "Bad." While the album hasn't done as well as "Thriller," its sales are still in the millions, and Michael's fans haven't been disappointed.

Michael Jackson has paid the price of fame. His childhood was spent rehearsing music and playing concerts. To dance and sing like Michael does takes constant hard work and dedication.

Michael is followed by newspaper reporters and photographers everywhere he goes. He has had to deal with rumors and distortions that are printed about him by magazines trying to cash in on his fame. Jackson has even taken to wearing disguises when he goes out in public.

But Michael's true love is music. He has sacrificed parts of his life to give his fans the absolute best that he can produce. His music is the most popular music in the world, and Michael generously shares his fame and his fortune. Michael visits sick children in hospitals and donates millions to charity. Michael Jackson has been an inspiration to untold millions. In the music world of the 80s, Michael Jackson's star shines the brightest.

PRINCE —
ROCK'S ROYAL HIGHNESS

No one is more of a symbol of 80s Rock than Prince. By fusing Funk, Punk, Soul and Rock into an irresistable dance beat, the Purple Prince of Rock invented a new musical sound. Prince's movies "Purple Rain" and "Under the Cherry Moon" have set styles and entertained millions. Prince showed them all how it's done, playing funk — with a capital F!

Prince was born Prince Rogers Nelson on June 7, 1960, in Minneapolis, Minnesota. His father and mother were both Jazz musicians, and they had a very stormy relationship. Prince's father left his mother when Prince was ten, leaving behind a piano.

Prince's mother remarried, but his stepfather treated him badly. Prince said his stepfather once locked him in his room for six weeks. The only thing in the room was a bed and a piano. Prince spent his time learning to play the piano. Before his 13th birthday, Prince had run away from home and lived variously with an aunt, his father and his friends. Prince finally settled down in the home of his best friend, Andre Cymone. During this period, Prince was very shy and kept to himself at school.

Prince, The Royal Rocker.

34

Influenced by Jimi Hendrix and Sly Stone, Prince formed a band called Grand Central with Andre, Morris Day and a few other friends. By the time he was sixteen, Prince was on his way to becoming a star, playing all his original songs in a band called Champagne.

TEENAGE STUDIO WIZARD

In 1976, a man named Chris Moon needed someone to help him write songs at his recording studio. He told Prince he would let him record for free if he wrote some music. Prince spent eight months recording the three songs he had written, playing every instrument himself.

Owen Husney, a friend of Moon's, took Prince's tape to the biggest record companies in Los Angeles. CBS, A&M and Warner Bros. all wanted to sign this teenage wonderkid. Prince insisted that he be allowed to produce all his own records, quite a demand from an unknown teenager. Warner Bros. consented, and Prince released "For You" in 1978. He had played all 27 instruments on the album himself!

Prince developed a cult following of people fascinated with his funky songs combining the twin themes of sex and loneliness. Prince released "Prince" in 1979, and "Dirty Mind" in 1980. "Dirty Mind" was a controversial album full of sexually explicit lyrics unheard of on a Rock record. Radio programmers refused to play the album which had Prince on the cover wearing only black underwear and a raincoat. Reviewers, however, were very impressed with the music on the album, a combination of white and black rock styles, a new sound termed "Techno-Funk."

LITTLE RED CORVETTE

After "Dirty Mind" was released, Prince went on the road, opening concerts for the Rolling Stones. In Los Angeles, Prince was booed by Stones fans that didn't understand his music, and he left the stage after only twenty minutes, under a hail of beer bottles.

After the Stones tour, Prince went into a frenzy of writing and producing. Prince wrote and produced an album for Vanity 6 and The Time, bands partly made up of his old Minneapolis friends. Besides all this outside work, Prince also released the albums "Controversy" and the double record set, "1999." Three singles were

Prince in Purple Rain.

released from the album "1999" — "Delirious," "1999" and "Little Red Corvette." "Little Red Corvette" was Prince's commercial breakthrough, fusing Funk and Punk and starting a trend that hundreds of bands would imitate. "1999" sold over 3 million copies.

PURPLE RAIN

All the big rock stars were pulling up in their limosines: John Couger, Quiet Riot, Stevie Nicks, The Talking Heads, Little Richard and Devo. They'd all come to honor the five-foot two-inch tall, 26-year-old Royal Funkster, clad in his trademark purple raincoat. The occasion was the premiere of "Purple Rain," a movie Prince had screenwritten, composed and starred in.

"Purple Rain" was Prince's multimedia triumph. The album sold 13 million in 1984, the score won an Oscar, and the video of the movie sold a cool one million. Prince was the biggest thing in Hollywood, and like Midas, whatever he touched turned to gold.

SIGN 'O' THE TIMES

Prince's success continued throughout the 80s. "Around the World in a Day," "Parade," "Sign 'O' the Times" and "Lovesexy" kept Prince Number

One on the music charts and at the center of controversy. Prince did the score for the blockbuster movie "Batman," and dozens of his videos have been in constant rotation on MTV. Vanity, Apollonia 6, Sheila E. and the Time are all musical planets circling around Prince's sun.

From his boyhood roots in Minneapolis to the stage and screen of Hollywood, singleminded dedication to music has made the Purple Prince part of Rock's Number One Royalty.

WOMEN WHO ROCK

The 80s were a time for women to regain a foothold in the world of Rock-n-Roll. Fueled by MTV and a new audience, Rock's women of the 80s sold records in numbers unheard of before. Tina Turner, Joan Jett, Chrissie Hynde, Heart, the Bangles and others proved that Rock-n-Roll wasn't just a mans game anymore.

MADONNA —
PRINCESS OF POP

Madonna Louise Veronica Ciccone was born on August 16, 1959, in Detroit, Michigan. She was the eldest daughter in a large family, and her mother died when she was six. Throughout her school years, Madonna loved to sing and dance.

Madonna, an overnite sensation.

In high school, Madonna twirled baton and starred in several plays. After six months in a Michigan college, Madonna moved to New York City to become a dancer. She arrived at Time Square with $35 in her pocket and a dream of stardom.

Madonna's early years in New York were lonely and disappointing. Living in cockroach infested apartments and working in a donut shop, Madonna waited for her big break. She met several musicians that taught her to play, and even played drums in several bands. In the early 80s, Madonna capitalized on the Punk explosion, and took to wearing torn tights, piles of jewelry, her prominent crucifix and of course her bare midriff, while hanging around New Yorks dance clubs.

In 1982, Madonna was signed by Sire Records, home of New Wave stars, the Pretenders and the Talking Heads. She had a hit with the funky "Everybody," and soon, wihtout a band and without touring, Madonna became a well-known singer in New York.

DESPARATELY SEEKING MADONNA

In 1984, Madonna released "Like a Virgin" and it rocketed to Number One, making Madonna a superstar. Madonna's natural acting ability shone brightly in the movie "Desparately Seeking Susan." Soon, malls all over America were filled with "Madonna-Wannabes" — teenage girls who dressed and looked like Madonna.

Seven Number One hits have been Madonna's legacy in the 80s. Millions of people all over the world have tuned in to Madonna's music in concert and on record. Madonna married actor Sean Penn in 1985 and divorced him in 1989. All of Madonna's relationships have been stormy, and this one was no exception. With the release of "Like a Prayer" in 1989, Madonna continues to top the charts.

Madonna struggled in New York for seven years before she got her big break. Her continued success proves that Madonna isn't just another pretty face, but a talented dancer and singer who can set trends and make great music.

U2 —
UNFORGETTABLE FIRE

One of the biggest bands of the 80s got their start in a simple manner. 14-year-old drummer Larry Mullen posted a note on the bulletin board at his school in Dublin, Ireland looking for musicians to form a band with. The Edge (David Evans) and Adam Clayton were the best guitarist and bassist to answer the ad. Mullen was in charge of the audition until Bono (Paul Hewson) arrived. Although he couldn't play or sing well, Bono had such an angry, uncompromising style, soon he was running the band. The group settled on the name U2, as in "you too" can join in the music.

Although the band couldn't play very well, they had spunk and excitement that attracted an audience. Bono mesmerized the audiences with his tough attitude. CBS Records signed the group in 1979 and released several singles in Ireland. Bono sent the singles to rock critics in England, and soon the critics were saying that U2 was the "next big thing." Island Records signed them in 1980 and soon U2 was on their way to the top.

BAND OF THE 80s

U2 developed a loyal audience by touring and recording self-important, socially aware albums. The critics said U2 would "save Rock-n-Roll" and in 1985, Rolling Stone Magazine called U2 the "Band of the 80s." When U2 released "Joshua Tree" in 1987, the single "With or Without You" stayed at Number One for three weeks. "Joshua Tree" gave the group their American breakthrough. And their serious, unsmiling faces even graced the cover of Time Magazine.

RATTLE AND HUM

1987 was the year of U2. They played to sellout crowds all over the globe and received a Grammy for the platinum "Joshua Tree." Their international tour is documented on the top selling album "Rattle and Hum" and in a motion picture of the same name. In 1989, Rolling Stone's readers elected them "Band of the Year" for the second year in a row.

As U2 matures, they are trying to put their angry, punk image behind them. They have a new-found preoccupation with American roots Rockers. Nowadays, U2 listens to the music of B.B. King,

U2 from Rattle and Hum.

Johnny Cash and Chuck Berry. With their socially aware music and their spiritual values, U2's loyal fans have put them at the top. U2 —the band of the 80s.

HEAVY METAL IN THE 80s

Long simmering next to superstars like Springsteen and Prince, several Rock-n-Roll bands have managed to sell millions of records by giving their rebellious teenage audience what they want to hear. Long ignored by radio stations and MTV, bands like Metallica, Motley Crue, Def Leppard and Guns n' Roses have risen to the top of the Rock heap. By bringing their music directly to the stage, the Metal bands sold so many records that they could no longer be ignored by the music industry. High energy, power Rock is still alive and well!

INTO THE 1990s

Time and space does not allow mention of all the great artists currently recording today. Of course, no one knows what will happen to people just cutting their first album today. Some of today's biggest stars might disappear from the scene

Guns N' Roses (L to R) Steven Adler, Izzy Stadin, Duff "Rose" McKagan, W. Axl Rose, Slash.

tomorrow or else go on to change history. You the listener decides who will succeed and who will not. As this book goes to press I'd like to mention some of the stars we'll be seeing a lot of in the early 1990's.

George Michael, Whitney Houston, Terence Trent D'Arby, INXS, Bon Jovi, Tracy Chapman, the Traveling Wilburys, Joan Jett, R.E.M., Fine Young Cannibals, Edie Brickell and the New Bohemians, Living Colour, XTC, and Michelle Shocked, to name but a few.

Right now, in some garage or basement, the future superstars of the 90s are honing their skills and writing music, waiting to take the world by storm. We are lucky to live in a time when so much soul-stirring music is available at our fingertips to fit our every mood. It's been said a million times — because it's true — "Rock-n-Roll will never die." Hallelujah!